75¢

D1361325

Flower Girl A to Z

Penelope Colville Paine

Paper Posie

For Rosemary Louise Wallington Paine

Paper Posie

Published by Paper Posie, Santa Barbara, CA
(800) 360-1761

Copyright © 2009 Penelope C. Paine
ISBN 978-0-9774763-3-6

To see all of Paper Posie's products for children at weddings
visit www.paperposie.com

Editor: Gail M. Kearns, www.topressandbeyond.com

Production: Cathy Feldman

Design and Typography: Peri Poloni-Gabriel, Knockout Design
www.knockoutbooks.com

Photography: Pages 8, 12, 28—Baron Spafford, www.baronspafford.com
Page 31—Dia Rao Photography, www.diaraophotography.com

Dress design: Page 8—Ann Buck, England
Page 25—David's Bridal
Page 32—Smocking by Joan Elizabeth Wallington

Special thanks to: Oliver, Alexa, Rosie and Miles Paine

1 2 3 4 5 6 7 8 9 10

Printed in China

This Book
Belongs To:

Chelsea

The Bride and
Groom Are:

Patty and Doug

Wedding Date:

June 11, 2011

A

is for A Wedding Day coming up soon

20

21

Wedding Day!

27

28

B is for the *Bride*, her *Bouquet* and *Balloons*

C is for a Cake and some Candy to share

D is for the beautiful Dress you will wear

E is for Exciting as the wedding day will be

F is for the Flowers you will carry carefully

G is for the Groom, lots of Gifts and the Guests

H is for Helping and doing your very best

I is for Invitations sent out in the mail

J is for Jewels in the bride's tiara and veil

K is for *Kisses* and hugs just for you

L is for Lots of Love

and a Little Luck too

M is for Music as you dance to the beat

N is for Nighttime and staying up for a treat

O is for Oh! how pretty you look

P is for Photos to keep in a book

Q is for Quiet

while the ceremony takes place

R is for Rings tied with Ribbons and lace

S is for Shiny new Shoes and your Smile

T is for Tossing the bridal bouquet in a while

$\mathcal{U}$ is for Umbrellas, but we hope it won't pour

V is for Violets, roses, daisies and more

W is for Wedding bells that ring out to say

X is for X-TRA fun and an extra great day

Y is for YOU, the best flower girl I know

Z is for ZZZs, your sleepy head on a pillow

Hope you enjoy being a Flower Girl...